Sacagawea and the Lewis and Clark Expedition

by
Sandra Taylor-Miller

AuthorHouse™
1663 Liberty Drive, Suite 200
Bloomington, IN 47403
www.authorhouse.com
Phone: 1-800-839-8640

First published by AuthorHouse 7/12/2007

ISBN: 978-1-4259-8358-1 (sc)

Printed in the United States of America
Bloomington, Indiana

This book is printed on acid-free paper.

authorHOUSE®

In loving memory of my Dad,

Robert Theodore "Dock" Taylor, Sr.

(10/02/1918 – 03/09/1985)

PREFACE

In July of 1998, the Secretary of the Treasury of the United States of America announced that the likeness of Sacagawea, a Shoshone Princess, would replace the image of Susan B. Anthony on the dollar coin. The new coin would be golden in color. The seventeen stars circling the Eagle on the reverse side represent the seventeen states of the union at the time of the Louisiana Purchase.

This announcement inspired me to want to learn more about this Native American woman. As a result of this research, I have developed a historical novel for young readers so they can become aware of the contributions made by Sacagawea towards the westward movement in the New World. In an attempt to bring history to life, I have blended historical facts with sympathetic characters. Shoshone Woman, the Great, ... Great Granddaughter of Sacagawea's son, Bazil, further inspired me by sharing information about Sacagawea with me.

In commemoration of the 200th Anniversary of the Lewis and Clark Expedition, the United States Mint issued a new series of nickels depicting President Thomas Jefferson on one side and the portrayal of events from the expedition on the other. The 2004 coins began with the Louisiana Purchase/Indian Peace Medal and ended with the keelboat in full sail which was designed and used by the explorers of the expedition. "The American Bison", honoring the Native Americans, and "Ocean in view! O! The joy!" depicting the explorers' first view of the Pacific Ocean, were issued in 2005. The last coin, "Return to Monticello", was issued in 2006.

Recently the United States Mint began a program honoring our Nation's Presidents by issuing new dollar coins featuring their images. Four new coins will be issued each year beginning with Washington, Adams, Jefferson and Madison in 2007. The Presidential coins will be issued in the order that the Presidents served. This is just one more way that the United States Mint has honored the people that have helped to mold our country.

Sandra Taylor-Miller

CONTENTS

"Have a windless day
and may your moccasins
never meet with sharp rocks."

Shoshone Woman,
Great, …, Great Granddaughter of Sacagawea

CHAPTER 1
Hide and Seek

"Seme', wahatche, bahaitee', watsewite, manegits, BIASECMOTE! Ready or not, here I come," shouted ten year old Huichu. Now it was time to find her older brother, Cameahwait (One Who Never Walks), and their friend, Jumping Fish, as they hid among the rocks and trees surrounding the village. She didn't care that she had cheated in her counting, jumping from five to one-hundred in one giant leap. The boys were always cheating when they played games and besides, she didn't get to play that often, and she really wanted to show the boys that she was a worthy opponent.

She quickly ran to the north side of the village, peaking behind the rocks and pines, always careful not to be spotted by the elders of the village. They would tell her father, the chief of the Shoshones, and he wouldn't like it. Games were not for Shoshone princesses or for any other girl in the tribe for that matter.

No boys in sight. Huichu worked her way around the perimeter of the village, checking behind every rock. Suddenly she heard a noise. It sounded like the chirping of a bird but something was not quite right. This bird had a giggle at the end of its song. She followed the sound, all the while searching behind every rock and tree along the path. She knew that she was on the verge of capturing her prey. She slowly crept toward the sound, careful not to step on a stick or make any other sound that would give her position away.

Just as she passed between two giant boulders, the two boys jumped out screaming, scaring the life out of poor little Huichu! Cameahwait doubled over in laughter as he shouted, "Did we frighten you Little Bird?"

Jumping Fish started chanting, "Little Bird, Little Bird, did we scare you Little Bird? Little Bird, Little Bird, did we scare you Little Bird?"

Huichu playfully pushed the two boys aside. "You didn't scare me at all. I was just pretending to be frightened to make you feel better," she retorted.

But her tormentors would give her no peace. They chanted over and over again,

"Little Bird, Little Bird,
Did we scare you Little Bird?
We jumped out from behind a rock
And gave Little Bird a great big shock!"

Huichu stuck out her tongue. That only made the boys determined to tease her even more. They pulled her hair and pushed her down on the ground. Huichu had just about had enough of this when she heard something that put real fear in her heart!

"Listen," whispered Huichu. "That must be Father and the other men returning from their hunt." The braves had been on a hunting expedition for the last three days. Food had been scarce for the Shoshones. It wasn't easy killing prey with bows and arrows. "I hope the hunt was a big success," she thought out loud. Her tummy was tired of the roots and berries that she had been living on for the past few weeks. Meat was much too scarce and valuable to waste on women. By the sound of the horses' hooves, Father's hunting party wasn't too far away.

Father must not find her here! How could she escape? Why wouldn't the boys stop chanting? Didn't they know what would happen to her if Father found her playing, especially with the boys? To make things even worse, she hadn't even started doing her chores for the day.

Huichu jumped up, brushed the grass and twigs from her clothes and ran back into the forest. With any luck, she would be back at her teepee before Father found out she was missing. As she ran towards her teepee, the boys ran in the opposite direction to greet the hunters. As they ran, they whooped and hollered wildly.

Huichu reached the teepee just as her mother came out to check the bison stew she had simmering over the fire. She had made it with leftover bison bones mixed with roots and berries that she had gathered in the forest. Sogobia, Mother Earth, was good to the Shoshones. She had provided for them since the beginning of time.

It was Huichu's job to gather twigs and limbs from the forest to keep the fire going. She looked at the place where the wood was supposed to be stacked. It was almost bare! How long had she been playing? It couldn't have been for that long! She knew what was in store for her when her father got home. Maybe he would be in a good mood, especially if the hunt had been successful. For the time being, however, she'd better gather what scraps of wood she could find so the fire would be able to burn throughout the night. She would worry about Father when he got there. But for now, she had better get busy restocking the woodpile.

CHAPTER 2
THE CHIEF RETURNS

All too soon, the Chief and his hunting party returned to the village. The hunt had been extremely disappointing for all of the braves. Father had only been able to shoot a couple of jack rabbits and a few doves with his bow and arrow over the last three days. That was just enough to feed the Chief and his son a few decent meals. They deserved the best morsels of food because they were the men of the family. Sadly, the other braves hadn't fared much better. Huichu and her mother, like the other women of the tribe, would have to continue on their diet of roots and berries.

Huichu rushed forward to take the horse from her father. "Welcome home, Father. I hope you had a good hunt." Her father responded to her greeting with a frown and a grunt. Not so good, she decided. She got the horse some hay and water, all the while trying to be very quiet and small so as not to draw attention to herself.

As her father approached the fire, Huichu pretended to be very busy with the horse, hoping that Father wouldn't notice her and the pitiful amount of wood in the pile. But luck was not with her. Her father was in a very bad mood, and the absence of wood for the fire did not make him any more pleasant.

The Chief dropped the game he was carrying on the ground in front of Huichu's mother and reached for his daughter. With one swift swoop, he picked her up and threw her on the hard, cold ground. Then he grabbed one of the larger sticks from the pile and began to swing. He hit her again and again and again. "Seme', wahatche, bahaitee', watsewite!" Huichu counted to herself. Would he never stop? Huichu wanted to scream out in pain, but she knew that would only enrage her father even more. She bit her lip and suffered in silence.

After venting his rage, her father sat down by the fire. He made a gesture which his wife knew meant that he was ready to eat. She took down one of the colorful bowls she had made from the clay the women of the tribe had gathered down by the river. She had shaped the bowls, painted them and hardened them in the coals of the fire.

She filled the bowl with stew and handed the steaming bowl of food to her husband.

He tasted it, made an awful face and glared at his wife. "This stew is terrible! How dare you serve such a nasty concoction to me, the mighty Chief of the Shoshones! There isn't even any meat in it. This is a poor excuse for a meal after I have been out hunting for three days!"

The Chief slapped his wife hard across the face and threw the stew into the fire, bowl and all. He gestured for his son, Cameahwait, to follow him. They headed off towards a group of men and young boys talking and laughing a few teepees away. There they would pass the pipe around and make plans for a big powwow where they would sing praises to Nato'se, Sogobia and the Great Mystery. They would decide what gifts they would give in order to ensure a good hunt the next time.

After they were gone, Huichu and her mother went into the buffalo skin teepee. Huichu was finally able to shed the tears that she had been holding in for so long. Her mother got out some of the salve she had made from the plants she had gathered in the forest. She rubbed the salve on the welts on Huichu's back. It did help to ease the pain in her back, but not the pain in her heart.

As Mother rubbed in the salve, she crooned a lullaby to her "Little Bird". She sang of the beautiful baby she had given birth to on that bitterly cold, wintry morning.

She sang of the little bird that sat and watched as the tiny infant let out her first cry, not much louder than the song of the little bird. She sang of how she had named her daughter Huichu, the Shoshone word for "little bird". The Chief didn't care what she named the child. It was just a girl and he, the Chief of the Shoshones, couldn't be bothered with the naming of a girl child! Besides, wasn't the fact that a little bird was there for the birth a sign from the Great Mystery that this child should have its name?

"Huichu, my sweet little bird," sang her mother. As Huichu shed the last of her tears, Mother stroked her long, dark hair. Such a beautiful daughter. Such spirit. Such intelligence. What a shame that she would suffer the same fate as her mother at the hands of an abusive husband.

"Mother, please tell me the story of how our people, the Shoshones, came into existence," Huichu pleaded. Mother told such wonderful Shoshone stories and they always made Huichu feel better. She quietly began telling Huichu the story of the beginning of the Shoshone people in the wonderful, musical voice that Huichu loved so dearly.

Once upon a time, long, long ago when snakes still had feet, there was a snake with extremely large feet. All the other snakes hated him just because he looked so strange with his huge feet. The other snakes drove the snake with big feet away from their land.

Snake walked and walked through the rain, sleet`and snow for many long, lonely days. He walked and walked until his huge feet were bruised and bleeding. He knew the end was near so he lay down by the river to wait for the Great Mystery to call him home.

As Snake lay there, the beautiful deer, E-se-ko-to-ye, took pity on him and carried him back to his lodge. There he fed him, washed him and bandaged his bleeding feet. He gently nursed the snake back to health. The deer taught Snake how to make nice, soft moccasins to protect his feet from the cold weather and the hard, rocky earth. Then he taught him how to make a lodge to keep out the cold winter winds. When Snake was better, he set out on his own again. He soon found a place deep in the forest to build his new home.

One cold, wintry morning just a few weeks after Snake moved into his new home, the Porcupine, Kais-kap, knocked on his door. He asked Snake for shelter since he had lost his own home in the recent rains. Remembering the kindness of the Deer, E-se-ko-to-ye, Snake took Kais-Kap in. In return for his kindness, Kais-Kap showed Snake how to take some of his quills and use them to weave a pattern on his moccasins to bring him good luck.

While out hunting one day, Snake came upon a very nice human family. He gave the Chief a pair of his beautiful, lucky moccasins as a token of peace and friendship. In return, the Chief allowed Snake to stay at his lodge for a few nights.

Snake soon observed that the Chief had an extremely beautiful daughter. He immediately fell madly in love with her. He knew that a lowly snake with big feet didn't have a chance with the beautiful princess. If only he could be a man instead of being a pitifully ugly old snake! He knew she could never fall in love with such a hideous creature.

Snake thought and thought about the beautiful young girl. He just couldn't get her out of his mind. One day as he sat dreaming of the girl, the medicine man, Mo'Ki-ya, walked by. Snake had a wonderful idea. He would ask Mo'Ki-ya if he had a spell which could change him into a human.

Mo'Ki-ya prayed about it to Natse'se, the Sun himself, who instructed him to build a fire and throw Snake into it. Mo'Ki-ya immediately gathered some wood and built a blazing fire. He said a prayer and threw snake into the flames. In just a few moments, a handsome young man stepped forward from the midst of the smoke. It was Snake! He had been purified by the fire. He had become a tall, muscular, handsome young man with normal sized feet.

It wasn't long before the Chief's daughter took notice of Snake and quickly fell deeply in love with him. They were soon married and over the years had many brave sons and beautiful daughters together. Their family continued to grow, giving Snake and his bride many grandchildren. Their family became a brand new tribe, the Shoshones, also known as the Snake People.

As her mother sat stroking her hair, Huichu once again asked her why the girls of their tribe had to work all of the time while Cameahwait and the other boys were only required to hunt, fish and play all day long.

Mother thought about Little Bird's question for a few minutes. She finally came to the conclusion that there was little she could say to justify this unfair treatment of the girls in her tribe to her daughter. After careful consideration, she finally said, "Huichu, my beautiful daughter, it is the Shoshone way that the women and girls do the menial tasks in our village. The men and boys need to be free from this drudgery so they can hunt and protect us from our enemies. We must make the clothes and teepees, prepare the meals, watch over the young, and care for the animals. The women and girls must collect the roots and berries, make the fires, and dress the animals that the men kill. Men are much too busy to worry about such trivial things."

"But why is it that the boys can get into all kinds of mischief and never get punished? I can't even think about doing some of the things they do without getting a beating," moaned Huichu. "Sometimes I don't even know why I am being hit!"

"Huichu, you know what the elders have to say about that! If the boys are punished or beaten, they will lose their spirit. Once the spirit is lost it can never be regained. A brave without spirit is of no use to our people," Mother replied. But her tone let Huichu know that she too felt that women were treated unfairly in their tribe.

As Huichu lay down on her grass mat that night, she dreamed of the many adventures she would have if only she were a boy! Little did she know that this was the last time that she would ever sleep surrounded by the warmth of the mother she loved, the brother she adored, or the father she looked up to but feared.

CHAPTER 3
THE RAID

Before the sun came up the following morning, Huichu was awakened by the screams and cries of her people. What was going on? "Wake up! Wake up! You must run into the woods and hide," shouted her mother. "Go quickly Little Bird! I will come and find you as soon as it is safe!"

Without asking for any details, Huichu jumped off her mat and ran into the forest as her mother had instructed. She hid behind the very same rock Cameahwait and Jumping Fish had hidden behind the day before during their game of hide and seek, but this time she wasn't playing a game! This time is was a matter of life and death! From her hiding place behind the rock, Huichu was able to see what all the commotion was about. She had heard many horrific tales of the Hidatsa warriors that had raided her village many years ago, killing and enslaving her people and stealing their horses. They had driven them from their hunting grounds on the plains where the buffalo were abundant to the mountains where there was little game. As an expression of their mourning, the members of the tribe had cut their hair short. Their long tresses had barely grown back to their original length when this attack occurred! These invaders matched the description of the ferocious warriors she had heard about in those horrible tales.

They swooped through her village burning and destroying everything in sight. Huichu wanted to hide her eyes from the horror they beheld but could not. Fear had too tight a grip on her. She stood frozen in place behind the rock, hoping beyond hope that her father and his warriors would defeat the Hidatsas.

From her vantage point, Huichu could see her Father and some of his warriors. They were putting up a valiant fight, but their bows and arrows and tomahawks were no match for the guns that the Hidatsas had gotten from the white men. As Huichu watched, her father was shot. He fell over and was still. Huichu swallowed the scream that was trying to escape from her throat. She must not give her hiding place away.

The bullets kept flying. She saw three more braves fall as well as a few women and several boys. She feared that her tribe was going to be totally destroyed and then the Hidatas warriors would search the area and kill those in hiding.

Huichu eventually was able to tear her eyes away from the battle. She crouched down at the base of the rock. There she sat for what seemed like hours, all the while listening to the screams of terror and pain as the people of her tribe were massacred.

Finally things began to settle down. Huichu's heart was almost beating normally when she heard a sound. Was it just a small animal scurrying around looking for cover, or was it her mother or brother coming to save her? What if it was a Hidatsa warrior coming to kill her or worse? Huichu dared not move a muscle, not even to breathe! When Huichu finally got up enough nerve to look down, she saw a deer hide moccasin, and then a tan, muscular leg. Who was it? What would he do to her? Before she was able to scream, a strong hand was placed over her mouth, drowning out all sound. She tried to bite and kick and scratch her captor, but he had too tight a grip on her.

"Little Bird, be quiet! The Hidatsas are still in the village. All of our people have been captured, found refuge in the forest and mountains, or been slaughtered by the Hidatsas," a hoarse voice whispered.

Huichu was finally able to squirm out of the strong arms that held her. She quickly spun around to face her attacker. She nearly fainted with joy when she realized that her captor was none other than her friend, Jumping Fish!

"We need to get out of here. Follow me," he whispered.

Without saying another word, Huichu and Jumping Fish began edging their way back to the safety of the woods. Just when they thought they were safe, they were stopped dead in their tracks by a lone Hidatsa warrior. There was no place to run and no place to hide. The strong, young Hidatsa brave was blocking their way. What was going to happen to them? Could they overpower him? Horrible thoughts of an uncertain future rushed through the minds of the young Shoshone boy and girl.

CHAPTER 4
CAPTURED

Huichu and Jumping Fish were petrified with fear! Would the Hidatsa warrior murder them on the spot or would he take them captive? They weren't sure which would be worse, being dead or being a slave to these savage people!

The warrior used gestures to communicate with the two children. He pointed and said something that although they couldn't understand the words, the meaning was obvious to both of them. The savage wanted them to return to the village.

Fearful for their lives, Huichu and Jumping Fish reluctantly headed back towards what remained of their village. That was the last place Huichu wanted to go after what she had witnessed happening there earlier that morning. But what choice did they have?

As they slowly approached the place that just the day before had been their home, the two children were horrified at the changes that had taken place. The buffalo skin teepees that had provided shelter for their families and friends were nothing more than smoldering mounds of rubble. Their belongings were scattered all over the ground.

Huichu spied a beaded bag that looked like the one her mother had made for her only a few months earlier. Observing that the Hidatsa warrior was looking in the other direction, Huichu quickly grabbed the bag and cradled it close to her heart.

As they proceeded through the destruction, only a handful of their people could be seen alive, standing in the corral where their horses had once been kept. Most of the people there were very old and had not been able to escape to the safety of the forest when the massacre began. Others were mere children, crying and searching for their mothers. Their lives had been spared only because they posed no immediate threat to their attackers.

Huichu searched the faces frantically in hopes of finding her mother or brother among the survivors. She already knew her father's fate. But the faces of the two she held so dear were nowhere to be seen. She did spy two other young Shoshone girls there among the survivors. They were her friends, Morning Star and Yellow Flower.

The bodies of men, women and children littered the village. Huichu and Jumping Fish were sickened by the horror of it all. They forced themselves to look to see if their loved ones were among the dead. They both said a silent prayer for the Great Mystery to accept the dead into the Great Beyond quickly and to protect those who managed to escape to the forest.

Once inside the corral with the other prisoners, Huichu dared to say her first words since they had been captured. "We must make our escape as soon as possible. The old ones will never make it back to the Hidatsas' camp alive. We must take Yellow Flower, Morning Star and the others with us and reunite with our people," Huichu whispered to Jumping Fish.

Jumping Fish was able to swallow his fear long enough to reply, "But how can we escape? They have guns and knives, and we have no weapons at all!"

"We must pray to the Great Mystery for a chance to escape, perhaps while the Hidatsas are asleep," wailed Huichu. In her mind she was angry. She was angry with her people for leaving her, she was angry with the Hidatsas for killing so many of her people but most of all, she was angry because she had been taught all of her life that boys had spirit, that boys were brave, that boys could save her! Well, this boy couldn't. He was even more frightened than she was!

CHAPTER 5

A CHANCE TO ESCAPE

The elderly Shoshones and a few of the smaller children quickly became too weak to walk, especially since the Hidatsa warriors didn't believe in wasting precious food and water on them. When they could no longer travel, they were left beside the path to meet whatever fate the Great Mystery had in store for them. It broke Huichu's heart to have to leave them, but she couldn't stay behind to help. Who would care for Morning Star, Yellow Flower and the other Shoshone children? And what would happen to that incompetent Jumping Fish if anything happened to her? Besides, their captors would never have allowed such a strong young girl to stay behind. So she trudged on day after day, week after week, doing everything within her power to keep the others safe.

Finally they arrived at the Hidatsa village. The children were almost immediately put to work, tending the gardens, cooking the meals, and tanning the hides of animals that the Hidatsa braves brought in from their hunts. The girls were used to this type of hard work because they had done it their entire lives. But poor Jumping Fish and the other boys suffered horrible. They had grown up in a world where they had no chores or responsibilities. All they had to do was hunt and fish and play all day. They hated the life they were being forced to live and schemed every day to find a way to escape.

Huichu, Yellow Flower and Morning Star eventually made friends with the other girls of the tribe. Huichu was now called Sacagawea, the Hidatsa word for Bird Woman. She was no longer a little bird. In the eyes of her captors, she was a woman even though at the time she was only twelve years old. Two years spent among the Hidatsas had forced her to grow up very quickly.

Sacagawea accepted the fact that she would never be with her people again. The only tangible item she had of her past life was the beaded bag that she had scooped up as she passed through her burning village that fateful morning long ago. It was indeed the one her mother had made for her. The beautiful red rose on the front was her mother's favorite pattern. She would keep it close to her heart forever. As far as the other things from her past, she was kept far too busy with chores and keeping Jumping Fish out of trouble to dwell on her losses.

Poor Jumping Fish spent every waking moment planning his escape. If only they would let him go into the woods alone to gather wood or berries, he'd be gone in a flash! But that would never happen. He was always under the watchful eye of one or another of the Hidatsa women.

Finally the opportunity to escape presented itself to the children. The braves came in one day from a very successful hunt. While everyone was admiring the kill, Jumping Fish drifted over to Sacagawea and whispered, "Now is our chance. Meet me behind the elder's hut tonight as soon as the moon rises."

The children knew that the women of the tribe would be busy that night preparing the meat from the hunt. Maybe, just maybe they would be able to slip away. Surely the braves would be too busy celebrating to notice a small group of children sneaking off into the night. They never paid any attention to those strange children anyway. The women who were usually responsible for watching them would be far too busy cutting and smoking the meat and curing the hides to notice. It was now or never!

As the moon began to rise in the dark, night sky, Jumping Fish headed for the elder's hut. Yellow Flower arrived moments later, as did the other children from the

Shoshone tribe. They waited and waited but no Sacagawea or Morning Star was anywhere to be seen! At last, they heard the muffled sounds of someone approaching. Was it the girls? Yes, they had finally come! But there was only one girl present. What was going on?

"What took you so long? Where is Morning Star?" Jumping Fish demanded.

"Morning Star is too sick to travel. I must stay with her. If I don't, who will take care of her? She is too sick to take care of herself and the Hidatsas will surely let her die," wailed Sacagawea. "You must go without us. When you find the rest of our people, come back for us."

Jumping Fish, Yellow Flower and the other children pleaded with Sacagawea to leave with them, but she refused. She felt too great a responsibility to care for Morning Star. Jumping Fish, Yellow Flower and the other children grudgingly vanished into the darkness as Sacagawea reluctantly returned to Morning Star and her life with the Hidatsas.

CHAPTER 6
THE HIDATSA TRIBE

Sacagawea and Morning Star lived among the Hidastas for three more years. During that time she grew to love many of the people of the tribe. She eventually grew accustomed to their strange circular lodges with mud roofs. How different they were from the buffalo skin teepees of her people. She learned to weave, creating beautiful blankets for the cold winter nights. She learned to work in the gardens, tending the corn, beans and squash – foods that she had never eaten before coming to the Hidatsa village. She found them to be much more to her liking than the roots and berries that had sustained her during her last months in the Shoshone village.

She taught the women of the Hidatsa tribe how to do beautiful beaded work just as her mother had taught her.

She did not, however, show any of them the bag that she kept close to her heart or how to make the beautiful rose pattern that was so dear to her mother. It was much too personal and special to share with anyone.

"Come," shouted one of the old women one fine spring morning. "Do you remember the man last fall who climbed on top of his lodge and made a vow to the Corn Spirit, Kudhutetash, whose name means Old Woman Who Never Dies? He told the members of the tribe that he wanted to live to see another season, to see his people become strong and prosperous, for the harvest to be bountiful and for our children to be as abundant as the flowers in the spring. Well, it is time to make preparations for the Corn Ceremony he promised to Kudhutetash. All winter long he has been collecting robes, clothing, horses and other items of value to be given away as presents or to exchange for medicine bundles. Now we must begin preparing for the feast."

The night of the festival finally came. Sacagawea and Morning Star excitedly watched as the Votary who had called for the Corn Ceremony the previous summer took a gift and a pipe to the man of supernatural strength. "Will you act as the Medicine Maker of the Corn Ceremony?" the Votary asked.

"Yes, I would be honored to serve as the Medicine Maker," he replied. "I will go now to the Singer who knows all the secrets and songs of the ceremony and make final preparations, offer him a robe and invite him to participate in the ceremony," he continued.

After smoking a pipe with the Singer, the Medicine Maker left the lodge so the Singer could begin dressing and painting himself in preparation of the festivities. After dressing in the new robe, he took a piece of charcoal and made three motions in front of his face. The fourth time he drew a mark across his face, singing "I am walking. I am walking."

These words meant that he was following the instructions the Old Woman Who Never Dies, Kudhutetash, had given to the first priest of the Corn Ceremony. Next he placed a necklace of yellow corn ears around his neck and sang, "Yellow, Yellow," which meant "Corn." He then took an ear of corn in his hand and chanted, "I am standing. I am walking."

The Singer placed a cap made from the head-skin of his medicine animal, the kit-fox, on his head. He continued singing his song, "Kit-fox is walking. Kit-fox is asking. Young Woman, your firesmoke I see; I am coming. It is here."

The guests were seated in the lodge dressed as birds which were thought to be the children of Kudhutetash. Medicine bundles were laid out in the center of the lodge. Incense was burned and the group left for the lodge of the Votary. The Medicine Maker, carrying the head of a deer, led the group with the Singer walking in the center. They passed the pipe back and forth four times as they walked.

A very fine buffalo skin had been spread as an altar in a place of honor in the lodge. The Votary and his wife were honored by the group. The bundles were rubbed against the Votary's wife to give her the strength and power which was contained in the medicine bundles.

Incense was burned again and all the participants rubbed their bodies in its ashes. The pipe was passed and the bundle was given to the Raven Man. The members learned the Raven songs. A plate of choice meat parts was placed in front of the altar. The Singer sang, "Madhidift, Ifdihkawahidith. I am walking in your path."

Sacagawea and Morning Star were totally absorbed in all of the things going on around them. They had never been allowed to participate in the ceremonies at home because that right was reserved for the men and boys. The women were kept busy behind the scenes preparing the food. The girls loved the chants, the dancing and the singing.

The Votary laid the bowl of food in front of the Singer. He sang, "I take: I offer: It is done."

The people started scrambling for the food, chirping like ravens, blackbirds and chickadees. The rest of the food was passed out to the other participants and to the spectators. The medicine bundles were passed out to their owners, and the Singer sang, "I am walking; I have finished. The land is green, the land is yellow, the land is gray."

The Medicine Maker then waved a bundle of sage towards the Four Winds and towards the door, ridding the lodge of evil spirits. He brushed himself with sage, took off his Kit-fox cap and necklace of corn, and washed his face. "Kadhakowift:huft-It is done: come," was the last song of the ceremony. It fulfilled the vow and asked the Corn Spirit to answer the prayers for a bountiful harvest.

The festivities lasted well into the night. The next day, everyone in the village rested. Sacagawea and Morning Star had a day of rest at last! They spent it talking about the families that they had not seen for so many long, lonely years and the new life they had made with the Hidatsa Tribe.

But the next day the girls were back to their old routine, working in the fields from the time the sun came up until the sun went down.

"I can't wait for the green shoots of corn to erupt from Mother Earth," Sacagawea exclaimed to Morning Star as they put the kernels of corn into the ground. "There isn't a more beautiful sight in the whole, wide world!"

But Morning Star did not share Sacagawea's enthusiasm. "I just wish we were finished with the planting. My back is killing me," she moaned.

Neither Sacagawea nor Morning Star would get to see the green shoots erupt from Mother Earth that spring. Before the corn had had time to sprout, Sacagawea and Morning Star were whisked away to yet another way of life, one that was even less pleasant than this one had been.

Chapter 7
The Mandan
Village

Sacagawea and Morning Star were rustled out of bed early one morning a few days after they finished planting the corn. "Get your things together. You are going on a journey," the elderly Hidatsa woman said.

The two girls quickly gathered their meager belongings. Sacagawea checked to make sure that the beaded bag was tied securely around her neck. She couldn't bear to lose this irreplaceable token of her mother's love.

When they emerged from their lodge, they were surprised to see a large group of Hidatsa men and women gathering in the center of the village. Their horses were loaded with blankets, corn, tobacco and other goods. From the excited chatter of the crowd, it didn't take Morning

Star and Sacagawea long to figure out that the Hidatsas were going to trade with their friends, the Mandans. Everyone was discussing the wonderful treasures that the braves would bring back on their return trip.

The group left the Hidatsa village a few hours later. For several days the party trudged along. "If they are going to trade with the Mandans, why did they bring us along," wondered Morning Star aloud. "They have never taken us anywhere before."

"Perhaps they want us to carry some of the goods back to the village when we return," replied Sacagawea. "You know how they come back every year with more and more treasures. Maybe they need our help and have just begun to trust us enough to go with them."

Little did they know the true intent of the Hidatsas. If they had, they would never have been so willing to go on this adventure.

After a few more days of steady travel, the group finally approached the Mandan village. The two young girls gasped at what they saw! The people of the village were different from any people they had ever seen or even imagined! They had hair that was as golden as the sun. Their skin was a pasty white. Where did they come from? Who were they? Why did they look so strange?

"Are they spirits?" whispered Morning Star. "They have yellow hair and pale, white faces! And look at their eyes. They are as blue as the sky!"

Sacagawea was also intrigued by the strange appearance of these people. Before she could reply to Morning Star's question, they were abruptly grabbed by two of the "Spirit People" who immediately took them off and put them into one of the strange structures that dotted the landscape.

They were left inside the hut for what seemed to be an eternity! The inside was dark and dusty. Their young imaginations were beginning to run wild. What in the world was going on? They waited inside the hot, airless huts for several long, miserable hours before they learned the harsh truth about their future.

Finally one of the Hidatsa braves that had accompanied them on the trip came to talk with Sacagawea and Morning Star. "You two have been traded to the Mandans," he said. "They need good strong women to work for them. Do as they ask, and you will not be harmed."

Then he turned around and left as abruptly as he had appeared. Morning Star began to cry. "Why have they done this to us? What did we do wrong? What will become of us?"

Sacagawea did all she could to calm her young friend down. "Maybe it won't be so bad. They don't seem to be evil even though they do look like spirits. We must do as we are told and all will be well," she said. She wished she was as confident as she sounded!

Sacagawea was right. Things were not good at this place. The girls worked hard in the fields from sunup to sundown. The Mandan language was very different from the Shoshone and the Hidatsa languages, so the girls did not always understand what was being said to them. They were beaten often for not immediately doing as they were told. They couldn't help it. They just didn't understand what was being asked of them. Life was indeed very difficult among these strange people.

These unusual people also had strange beliefs. They talked of a woman giving birth to a son even though she had never been with a man. They called the child Jesus. He grew up and exhibited very magical abilities. He could heal the sick and feed the hungry. Every winter they had a celebration in his honor on the date of his birth.

They also told of a great flood. One man and his family built a huge canoe that they called an ark. When they finished building the giant canoe, they placed a pair of every known plant and animal on board. When they were finished loading the animals, it started to rain. It rained for forty days and forty nights, flooding the Earth and killing everything that was not safely on board the ark.

Where in the world did they get these strange ideas? Everyone knew that the Great Mystery was the only deity capable of performing such miracles.

"I hate it here!" screamed Morning Star one day as they were making their way to the fields for yet another day of back-breaking labor. "The people are mean, and I am always tired and hungry. I wish we could escape!"

"Don't be foolish, Morning Star. We wouldn't get a hundred yards away before the 'Spirits' caught up with us. Then they would punish us," said Sacagawea. "Just do what they say. The Great Mystery has always taken care of us. He will provide for us again. Now, get back to work. They are watching us."

Little did the two girls know, but their lives were about to change again. Their fate this time would be far worse than slavery to the Hidatsas and the Mandans had ever been.

CHAPTER 8
SACAGAWEA MARRIES

"I won! I won!" bellowed the short, fat, balding middle-aged man. "I will take the two standing by the wall. Are they Shoshone? I hope so because the Shoshone squaws make the best wives. They know their place in the home! No talking back from them!"

Sacagawea and Morning Star were the two to whom he referred. How she hated the little man that spent so much time in the Mandan village. She had had to ward off his advances more than once since she had been there. Now she belonged to him, won as a prize at a game of chance! How would she bear it? She loathed the very sight of him.

Everyone in the village was sick of his bragging and rough ways. "Chief of Little Village" was the not so complimentary name by which he was known by the Mandans. The "Little Village" they made reference to was the village of his many "wives" whom he beat regularly. It made him feel important to belittle the women. He was as sorry a man as had ever lived.

But like it or not, she now belonged to him and must do as he said. "Mother, please be with me in my hour of need," Sacagawea muttered under her breath. She clasped the beaded bag closer to her heart. What would she do? And poor Morning Star was hysterical! It took Sacagawea many minutes to calm her friend down.

After a few more games of chance, Toussaint Charbonneau, part Iroquois Indian and part French-Canadian, came to claim his prize. He smelled worse than the animals that he captured for his fur trading business! He wasted no time in snatching Sacagawea and Morning Star up and taking them back to his lodge. He was not gentle, taking what he wanted from each of the girls and then quickly passing out. Such snoring!

Sacagawea had never felt so dirty in her whole life. Lye soap and water couldn't wash away his stench! How would she bear this new burden that had been thrust upon her? Tears poured down her face as she watched the nasty little man sleep.

At least she wasn't the only one he came to in the night. He had several "wives", a few being Shoshone like Sacagawea. The only good thing about this living arrangement was that the women were able to talk to one another during the day as they did their chores.

"I hate that little toad," one of them said one morning. "He treats his dogs better than he treats us."

"He's such a whiner. He throws a temper tantrum whenever he doesn't get his way," Morning Star responded.

"I pray every night that he will not make it home," said one of the other "wives". "I think that just maybe he will say something or do something to one of the warriors, and they will take him out!"

Sacagawea didn't wish him any harm, but she knew what the other women were talking about. He owned them just as he owned his dogs. But the dogs were treated more humanely. She too dreaded his appearances in the night but preferred not to make any comments.

The reference to dogs reminded Sacagawea of a story her mother used to tell her about when the world was ruled by dogs and decided to share it with her friends. It would help to relieve the boredom of their work and put a smile on their faces. It would also take their minds off their hateful husband for a few minutes. She began the story in her soft, musical voice.

Long, long ago the world was ruled by dogs. There were many different sizes, shapes and breeds of dogs. But they all had one thing in common-each had a beautiful tail that matched his or her coat. And each one of them thought his tail was the most magnificent tail of all. They spent many long hours admiring their reflections in the river which ran by their teepees. Before long the inevitable happened! They began to fuss and fight among themselves about who had the most beautiful tail. There were howls of outrage as they began insulting each other. This led to growling, gnashing of teeth and fighting among all the members of this Canine Village.

The Great Mystery couldn't help but hear the ruckus going on down below. It hurt him to hear the rulers of his beautiful world fighting over something as insignificant as a tail. He thought and thought about the problem and finally had an idea that might just solve it. He would dress up as Brother Bear and pay the dogs a visit. He didn't want them to know that he was getting involved in their business.

When the Great Mystery arrived, all of the dogs thought it was just Brother Bear from the island in the middle of the river paying them a visit. They listened intently as he invited them to a powwow and a great feast over on his island on the night of the next full moon. The dogs were intrigued with this proposition and began discussing it among themselves. They excitedly began making plans for the powwow.

Suddenly one of the vainer dogs realized that there was a major problem with going to the powwow. "We can't go to the powwow! It is on the island and in order to get there, we would have to swim across the river. If we swim, our beautiful tails will get wet," he wailed.

All of the other dogs quickly agreed that they just would not be able to attend the party. It would never do to get their beautiful tails wet! "Is it possible to have the powwow over here?" they inquired when the Great Mystery, still dressed as Brother Bear, dropped by to make the final arrangements a few days later.

Knowing that this would compromise the intent of having the event on the island in the first place, Brother Bear quickly responded, "Oh no, everything is already set up on the island for our powwow. I knew how important your tails were to you so the Great Mystery and I have discussed it. He has decided that for just this once, each one of you may pull off your tail and hang it over there on the bushes where it will stay nice and dry until you return from the powwow," he said.

All of the dogs quickly agreed that this was a good idea and excitedly prepared themselves for the party. The night of the full moon finally arrived and all of the dogs gathered by the edge of the river, admiring their magnificent tails just one more time before hanging them on the bushes. Tentatively, one of the braver dogs tugged on his tail. Just as they had been promised, his tail popped right off and it didn't even hurt! He carefully draped it over one of the branches of the bushes close by and dove into the river. The other dogs followed suit, each one being careful to hang his or her tail in just the right spot so it would stay safe and dry.

What a day they had! There were contests where they could showoff their skills as well as foot races. They even had a howling contest! They ate and ate the delicious traditional foods until their stomachs were dragging the ground! The dogs were so busy enjoying themselves that not once did any of the dogs even think about their tails. The Great Mystery was pleased. His plan was working.

It was almost dark and time for the dancing to begin when all of a sudden, there was a great streak of blinding light followed by a tremendous "Boom!" The poor dogs were so frightened that they immediately stopped what they were doing and stared in horror. Then it happened again. This time it was even closer! Their day of fun had come to an abrupt halt! Suddenly it dawned on them. Thunder and lightening was usually followed by rain! Their beautiful tails were going to get wet! They had to get back across the river and reclaim their tails before they were messed up by the rain.

En masse, the dogs leapt into the river and swam just as fast as they could to the opposite bank. When they reached it, they ran as fast as they could to the bushes, grabbed a tail, stuck it on, and ran for their teepees! As they began drying themselves off, they realized that in their haste, they had grabbed the wrong tails! A great big dog had a tiny little tail and a sleek dog had a fuzzy, curly tail! A curly haired dog found that she had a long, rat-like tail and another one found that his tail was no longer thick and long but was instead skinny with a funny curly cue at the end. They thought they looked ridiculous!

All of the dogs moped around for days, embarrassed by the tails that they now had. How silly they looked. They stopped admiring themselves in the river and went about their days doing their chores as quickly and as quietly as possible. The bickering stopped. The Great Mystery was pleased. His plan had worked.

The Great Mystery came to visit again, but this time he came as himself. "I have come to see how you are enjoying your new tails," he said. The dogs hung their heads in shame, secretly hoping that the Great Mystery would give them back their own beautiful tails. Reading their minds, the Great Mystery shook his head and said, "I am sorry but I can't give you back your perfect tails. If I did, I am afraid that you would become vain again and all of the fussing and fighting would resume. I can't have that so you will just have to be satisfied with what you have," he continued.

"Oh yes, be sure to tell your children and your children's children what happened on the night of the Powwow of the

Full Moon," he ended. *With that, he left the dogs with their misery.*

This event happened a long, long time ago. Many generations have come and gone but to this very day, whenever you see two dogs approach each other on the street, they sniff one another's tail. They aren't being rude, they are just trying to see if the other dog has the tail that once belonged to his or her ancestor!

All of the "wives" had a good laugh at Sacagawea's story. How wonderful it was to have someone to entertain them during their long, lonely days.

Chapter 9
Joining the Expedition

"But gentlemen, you can't imagine how important I could be as an interpreter on your journey. I speak both French and Sioux. Your other interpreter speaks only French and English. How do you think you will be able to communicate with the Indians you will surely meet on your journey? You will need my assistance," Charbonneau informed Meriwether Lewis and William Clark.

In a treaty signed on April 30, 1803, President Thomas Jefferson had purchased more than 800,000 square miles of land extending from the Mississippi River to the Rocky Mountains from France for about $15,000,000. This land was known as the Louisiana Purchase and it doubled the size of the United States. Little was known about this new land except the fact that Indians lived there and a few daring white trappers had ventured into the area.

Lewis and Clark had been commissioned to find a water passage through the northwest by President Jefferson. Jefferson believed that the explorers would find prehistoric creatures like woolly mammoths along with huge volcanoes in this new land. He also believed that they would find a waterway which would allow boats to sail from the Missouri River all the way to the Pacific Ocean, only stopping occasionally to travel overland. The Corps of Discovery, the official name of the expedition, had camped for the winter at Fort Mandan, North Dakota. Charbonneau had heard about the expedition in the Mandan village and wanted a piece of the action.

Neither Lewis nor Clark really liked this annoying little man but what he said held some truth. They would need someone to deal with the various Indian tribes they met on their journey. That individual would need to be familiar with their customs and languages.

"Besides, I have a Shoshone wife. She can help us when we get to the Rockies. She grew up in that area. She not only speaks Shoshone, she speaks Mandan and Hidatsa as well. She would really be an asset when we pass through Indian territories. We will also need horses to continue our journey, and the Shoshones will be our only means of getting them. Do you really think they will deal with you? No way," the nasty little man admonished. He didn't bother to tell them that the wife he was talking about would be giving birth to her first child in a few short months. It should arrive just before the expedition proceeded on their journey west and he was afraid they would be unwilling to risk the life of a small infant and its mother.

"He does have a point," Lewis said. "It may be helpful to have someone with us who can speak both Sioux and Shoshone."

"Having a woman with us would probably be beneficial by letting the Indians know we are friendly. Aggressors would not have a woman with them," Clark added. "A woman with a party of men is a token of peace to the Indians. They know that a war party would never travel with a woman."

So it was settled. Charbonneau and his wife, Sacagawea, would accompany them on their trip.

The next few weeks were spent in preparation for the long journey which lay ahead of them. The white men and the Mandans hunted buffalo together, preparing some of the meat to help sustain them through their long journey to the west coast. The white men provided medical assistance to the natives when it was needed. They sharpened axes, mended hoes and repaired firearms for the Mandans. In exchange, the Mandans helped them to learn about the strange plants and animals in this new land. They also gave them corn and tobacco.

On February 11, 1805 one of Charbonneau's "wives" approached Lewis. "Hurry, Sacagawea's baby is coming! She is in trouble and we need your help!" she exclaimed excitedly. When he arrived at the Charbonneau home, he found Sacagawea writhing in pain.

Lewis was shocked because he hadn't realized that the "wife" Charbonneau was planning to carry on their journey was pregnant. However, since he couldn't change that fact, he had to do all he could to help her. He needed a healthy woman to accompany them on their trip west in order to secure the food and horses they would need in order to proceed safely.

"Give me that container of crushed rattlesnake rings and some water," Lewis told the excited woman. "It will help speed up the delivery." This was the standard medicine at that time for difficult deliveries.

The medicine must have worked because Jean-Baptiste Charbonneau was born about ten minutes after the administration of the medicine. The birth was very difficult for the young girl. Conditions during his birth were unsanitary to say the least. Sacagawea was close to death. Her fever raged, and for several days she was delirious. The other "wives" had helped to deliver the baby. Now they took care of both Sacagawea and the infant.

Her husband was of no use at all, just stopping by long enough to see that is was indeed a boy and to inform the "wives" of its name. No sissy girls for him! He could care less if Sacagawea lived or died. He would replace her with another "wife" without a second thought.

Slowly, Sacagawea began to heal. Morning Star had been able to secure some more of the white men's medicine from Captain Lewis. It seemed to help.

When she was strong enough, Sacagawea asked to see her child. One look into his beautiful eyes was the best medicine in the world for the new mother. She would become strong and get well for her son.

"Isn't he beautiful?" she asked the other "wives". "I will teach him to be a good, caring, loving person, not a lying cheating little weasel like his father!"

The other "wives" agreed that Baptiste was indeed a beautiful child. They all loved and cared for him as if he was their own.

As Sacagawea regained her strength, Baptiste became a plump, happy baby. His dark, shiny eyes followed every movement the women made as they went about doing their chores. He was interested in everything around him and he kept Sacagawea and the others busy day and night.

All the while, Sacagawea was busily getting together the items she would need for their long journey west. Traveling with a small baby would not be easy. "I can't get Toussaint to do anything. He is totally worthless," she complained to the other "wives", something she rarely did.

The other "wives" helped Sacagawea in any way that they could. They made clothes for the baby, they put together items Sacagawea would need in order to cook meals on the journey, and they gathered plants and herbs that she could use to season their food and some that she could use to make medicines. They could hardly wait! Their hateful, lazy "husband" would be gone for a year or more. "We'll have to work hard in order to feed ourselves, but at least we will not have to wait on that little weasel for a while," they exclaimed excitedly.

All too soon, the spring thaw was upon them, and it was time to leave. Sacagawea said a tearful good-by to her new family, put Pomp into his cradle board, strapped him to her back, and headed out to join the rest of the party. The others helped her carry the parcels they had worked so hard to put together for the trip.

As she approached the group, she noticed that a heated discussion was going on between her husband and the leaders of the expedition. "If you can't accept these demands," her husband was screaming, "then you will lose two of your most important interpreters!"

Lewis and Clark walked away. They looked over the list of demands in disbelief.

"Can you believe this?" Clark asked. "He thinks he is too good to do labor of any kind, he doesn't want to have to stand guard, and if the mood strikes, he thinks he can leave the expedition any time he wants and take whatever and whomever he needs in order to survive! This is totally unbelievable! Who does that little toad think he is?"

"But we do need him to help us communicate with the Indians. And we need his Shoshone 'wife' to help us once we get to the Rockies. Our mission will not be able to proceed past that point without her contacts with the Shoshone tribe. We are going to need their horses. Let's just go along with his demands. He would never leave the expedition once we get out in the wilderness," replied Lewis. "However, let's not agree just yet and give him a little time to think about it. He really wants to go on this expedition."

"Alright men, finish loading the boats!" shouted Lewis. "We leave in one hour!"

Lewis was right. After thinking about what he had said, Charbonneau decided that perhaps he had spoken too quickly. He went back to the Captains and apologized, modifying his demands to make them more palatable.

"Thank you for coming to your senses," Clark told Charbonneau. "We really do need you and your wife as interpreters on our journey. Just put your supplies in that boat over there."

"You heard him, woman! Put the supplies in the boat," Charbonneau screamed at Sacagawea. She rushed to do as she was told. She didn't want to make Charbonneau mad this early in the trip.

Seeing what was going on, Clark looked at Lewis in disbelief. "I knew I didn't like that man. Can you believe he makes her do all the work while he sits around whining and complaining? I'm used to men doing the physical labor. Women shouldn't have to lift those heavy packages!"

That was just the beginning. As time passed, Clark observed many events that eventually led up to his total loathing of Toussaint Charbonneau.

Chapter 10
The Journey West

On April 7, 1805, the thirty-three explorers boarded two pirogues and six smaller dugout canoes and started their historic journey west on the Missouri River. Everyone was excited about this trip into a world where only a few daring white men had ever set foot. The crew, hand picked by Lewis and Clark, consisted of carpenters, blacksmiths, woodsmen, a boatman, millers, a gunsmith, navigators, tailors and a one-eyed French fiddle player. Most of these men had more than one job on the journey. Of the thirty-three explorers, there were only five civilians. Charbonneau, Sacagawea and George Drouillard were interpreters for the expedition, and York was Lewis's black manservant. And of course there was baby Baptiste, but he was just along for the ride.

Sacagawea quickly found out what the trip was going to be like for her. Her husband made her take care of packing and unpacking each time they stopped. She had to build the fire, set up the camp, forage for food, cook, sew, and mend and clean the clothes for her family. She did this in addition to caring for a very young baby.

After a few days, Sacagawea longed for home. At least there she could get a little peace, and there was always someone for her to talk to. Her husband was the only one that spoke Shoshone in the entire group. However, he was so busy showing off for Lewis, Clark and the others on the expedition that he barely acknowledged her presence. When he did, it was to give her instructions on yet another chore she needed to do. Sacagawea knew that if she was going to survive this trip, she would have to make some changes as to what her responsibilities would be. However, she had no idea how to begin making those changes. She had been raised knowing a woman's place, and it didn't include telling the men what she would and wouldn't do.

"Charbonneau, bring that squaw over here and get her to tell me what kind of plants I have found," Meriwether Lewis yelled one day during the second week of the trip. Part of his job with the expedition was to take samples and catalog plants and animals that they discovered along the way. He didn't notice the hurt in Sacagawea's eyes when he said the word "squaw". It was the only word that the white man had said the entire journey that she had understood.

Charbonneau signaled for Sacagawea to come. When she got there, he pointed to the plant that Lewis was referring to. Sacagawea looked at the plant and began digging it up. "The root of this plant is edible," she said. That particular plant became a staple among the explorers during their trip. She then proceeded to tell Charbonneau the names of other plants in the area.

Lewis quickly drew and labeled the plants and their Indian names in his journal. "This one makes a salve that helps to heal cuts," Sacagawea continued. She became misty eyed as memories of her family flashed before her eyes. This was the same kind of plant her mother had used to make a salve to treat the welts her father had put on her back when he beat her. "These can be boiled in water to make an herbal tea which can help to settle stomach aches," she said, pointing to yet another plant.

Lewis was amazed at the knowledge of plants that Sacagawea possessed. Every night on the journey, Lewis and Clark would sit together for a couple of hours, discussing the events of the day. They would map out their journey using the placement of the stars to help them locate their position. They would write notes detailing incidents that occurred during the day and naming places and people they had encountered along the way. During their discussion that night, Lewis mentioned the expertise of the "squaw" in the names and uses of plants.

"What did you say? You called her a 'squaw'! Do you know what that means? It's an Indian word for prostitute! Sacagawea is not a prostitute! Never call her that again. She is much too valuable to us to be insulted that way," screamed Clark.

"I'm sorry," Lewis said. "I didn't know that the word 'squaw' meant that! How awful it must have made that poor girl feel."

From that day forward, the word "squaw" was never used by the men in the camp in reference to Sacagawea. They were all gaining a new respect for the quiet, gentle woman that worked so hard to keep things running smoothly on their journey west.

Chapter II
The Grizzly Bear

On April 29, the party entered land that is now known as Montana. They were amazed at the abundance of game. Buffalo, deer, elk and antelope were prolific in this new land. Lewis was elated. "What a wealth of wildlife we have here. My pen can hardly write fast enough to record all the different species I've seen today," he exclaimed to other members of the party.

Sacagawea was busily naming and relating all pertinent information about each of the plants to Charbonneau in Shoshone who was in turn translating to Drouillard in French. Drouillard then repeated the information to Lewis in English. It was a lengthy, time consuming process but it was the only way that Lewis could get the information that he needed.

Suddenly a loud roar was heard. It made the hairs on the back of the explorers' necks stand on end. The ferocious growling was accompanied by the excited yelping of Lewis's large black dog, a Newfoundland named Seaman. The group jumped up to see what the excitement was all about. They froze in terror as they saw the invader. It was a huge grizzly bear, not yet fully grown but already weighing in at over 600 pounds.

The explorers had had previous experience with this type of bear. They had found that if they didn't shoot it in just the right place, the bear would charge. It usually took several shots just to bring a bear down. Just a few days earlier, two men had attempted to kill one. They had shot it several times but the bear continued charging. They finally had to toss their weapons into the bushes and leap into the cold, raging river just to escape! Therefore the group was very aware of the danger they were in.

Sacagawea instinctively pulled Baptiste closer to her, trying to protect him from the raving animal that stood before them. The situation was desperate. What were they going to do? Not one person in the group was armed except for the small knives they were using to dig around the plants. They had not even thought about bringing weapons on this mission to observe and identify plants. Plants weren't dangerous. And besides, they were just a few yards away from their camp. But with the grizzly between them and the camp, they had just as soon of been thousands of miles away!

"Don't move a muscle," Lewis whispered. "Once the bear sees that we are not food, and that we are not a threat, he will leave us alone. However, if anyone moves or makes a sound, he will charge."

The three men, one woman and a young child remained motionless as the bear sniffed the air. He was just looking for food and the explorers didn't have any food with them. He turned and started back into the forest.

Suddenly, Little Baptiste let out a cry. The bear stopped short, turned around slowly, and looked. The baby was getting hungry, and he let out another whimper. The bear charged!

Before the bear took another step forward, a shot was heard. Then another. It took both shots from York's rifle to bring the large bear down. York, Clark's black manservant, was luckily working on a canoe close by when he heard the ruckus and came over to investigate. When he saw the bear, he knew that the lives of his friends depended on the accuracy of his shot. A bad shot would just infuriate the bear even more. He aimed carefully, shot and luckily killed the huge grizzly with the first shot. He fired the second shot just in case the first one didn't do the trick.

Sacagawea emitted a sigh of relief as the huge bear fell forward. She just knew it had been heading straight for her and her child. She hugged Baptiste even closer, and he cried even louder.

Charbonneau didn't have to play dead in order to fool the bear. He had fainted dead away at the first sign of trouble. This earned him yet another nickname, Fallen Bear. Like his other nicknames, this one was not meant to be a compliment!

The men dressed the grizzly bear. They cleaned it and saved the fur to use for blankets and coats when the cold winter winds returned. The fat was stored in pouches made from the bear's bladder and intestines to be used for frying foods later in the journey.

That night they all feasted on grizzly bear steaks and sat around the fire talking of the great adventure they had had that day. "Fallen Bear" went to bed early which was a blessing for him because he became the brunt of more than one joke that evening.

CHAPTER 12
OVERBOARD

On May 14, the Corps of Discovery found themselves close to Crooked Creek. The food supply was quickly becoming depleted so Lewis, Clark and some of the others in the scouting party went ahead of the others and were on shore doing some hunting. They had been on shore for only an hour or so when the wind began to pick up. They knew that the others were just around the bend in the river and that the wind would make the passage extremely dangerous for them. They shouted and shot their guns into the air trying to get the attention of the others, but it was to no avail. The others did not heed their warning if indeed they had even heard it.

Sacagawea, Little Baptiste and Charbonneau were traveling on one of the boats. Sure enough, when they went around the bend in the river, the wind picked up. Charbonneau, one of the poorest steersmen in the entire expedition, was trying to steer the boat. As luck would have it, a gust of wind caught the boat broadside and flipped it over. Everything and everyone in it was dumped overboard into the cold, rushing water.

Charbonneau immediately headed for shore. "Get back there and help Sacagawea," the men yelled from the shore. But Charbonneau was too intent on saving his own hide to worry about his wife and son. He continued swimming to safety, leaving Sacagawea on her own to get herself and the baby to the river's edge.

Sacagawea, with baby Baptiste still strapped to her back, waded waist deep in the freezing water. She grabbed parcels to keep them from floating away. In those parcels were maps, medicines and supplies that they would need in order to continue on their journey west. Books, clothing, a magnet, a microscope and the captain's journals were also stored in those parcels that Sacagawea retrieved.

It took every ounce of strength Sacagawea had to bring herself, her baby and the parcels safely to the shore. When she got there, her husband was stretched out on the grass, breathing hard and acting as if he had done all of the work. Sacagawea had the urge to kill the little toad, but she knew she couldn't. Besides, she would have to stand in line because everyone else that had witnessed his behavior that day wanted to kill him too!

That night, Lewis and Clark held a great feast in honor of Sacagawea. They had been fortunate enough to shoot some game for their dinner. Captain Clark stood up to make a toast. "Sacagawea," he began, "It is with our deepest gratitude that we honor you this night. Without your quick thinking and bravery, we would have lost many articles that are necessary for the success of our journey. I would like to present you with this small token of our appreciation." With that, Captain Clark presented Sacagawea with a beautiful belt of sky blue beads.

Not to be outdone, Lewis made the next toast. He said, "Sacagawea, we can never repay you for what you have done for us on this journey. Today is just another example of how you have come through in our hour of need. I would like to name a river in your honor. From this day forward, this tributary of the Missouri River will be known as Sacagawea, or Bird Woman's River."

Sacagawea had never been so excited in her whole life. She didn't know what to say because she had never received any praise before. She may not have known much about it, but she certainly did enjoy it! For the first time in her life, people were looking at her as if she was a real person. With tears of joy in her eyes, she thanked the men profusely for the honors they had bestowed upon her.

As he had done so many nights before, the one-eyed fiddler brought out his fiddle and the dancing began. He played late into the night, lifting the spirits of all of the explorers even further.

As Sacagawea walked towards her tent that night, she felt like a new woman. She was so excited and happy. She kept admiring the beautiful belt and thinking about having a river named after her. What an honor!

Her joy was short-lived. Jealous of all the attention his wife was getting, Charbonneau became angrier and angrier by the minute. He wasn't able to ignore the speeches because he had to translate every word that was spoken! He was also aware of all the derogatory jokes going around about him, so Charbonneau decided that it was high time to teach Sacagawea a lesson. She hadn't had a good beating lately and besides, beating up on women always made him feel better.

As she approached the tent, Charbonneau attacked her. He started by calling her ugly names. When this gained no response, he started slapping her around. Years of abuse had taught Sacagawea that showing no response at all was the best way to handle a man when he decided it was time to attack. She crumpled onto the ground, protecting herself as best she could. He finally stopped, but not before leaving his mark upon her. Sacagawea had bruises on her body, a shiny black eye and a busted lip by the time Charbonneau finished with her.

The next morning at breakfast, Captain Clark took one look at Sacagawea and decided this behavior had to stop. He immediately went to Charbonneau's tent, pulled open the flap, and hauled the little man out by his heels. "You do not hit women, you deranged creature! Look at Sacagawea's face," he yelled.

"But I didn't do anything to her," Charbonneau screamed in his defense. He was frightened because Clark was really mad. "She must have tripped and fallen on a rock."

"Don't insult my intelligence with that lie," shouted Clark. "If you ever dare to touch a hair on her head again, you will have me to deal with!" he screamed.

From that day on, Charbonneau made sure that if he did hit his wife, he didn't leave any visible marks for Captain Clark to see. Sacagawea was eternally grateful to Captain Clark for his intervention. A special bond was beginning to form between the Shoshone woman and the captain of the Corps of Discovery.

Chapter 13
The Great Falls
of the Missouri

On June 13, Lewis was ahead of the group with a scouting party when they discovered a beautiful sight – an area which he named the Great Falls of the Missouri. "This is the grandest sight I have ever beheld," he exclaimed to his men. Little did he know at that time that those spectacular falls would slow the expedition down for at least a month.

After searching for a way to cross the falls, the group decided to set up camp. They realized it would take time for them to construct the sleds to haul their canoes and supplies around the five cascades of water that made up the Great Falls. Sacagawea rushed around setting up the tent, starting the fire, nursing the baby and preparing the food. Her lazy husband just sat by idly gossiping with a group of men as they continued working.

The men fished as their leaders worked on a plan of action for getting over the falls. "Look at this strange fish I caught," one of the men shouted. Sacagawea was called over. She identified it as a cutthroat trout, a new species for Lewis to catalog in his journal. Others threw in their lines and quickly began pulling in a number of the creatures. They had tired of the beavers that they had been eating for quite a while even though beaver tails were quite delicious.

That night Sacagawea helped the men clean and cook the fish in the fat they had saved when they killed the big grizzly bear. "I believe that these are the best fish I have ever eaten," the men said as they wiped the grease from their mouths. They ate until their bellies were stuffed.

They decided to catch and dry some of the fish the next day. They had no idea what would be available on the next leg of their journey. Besides, they were going to be in the area for a while and they'd just as soon do something constructive while they waited.

Clark began to worry about Sacagawea. She wasn't acting like herself. He had noticed it as she was helping to cook the fish the night before. She had hardly eaten a thing and she kept rubbing her stomach as if she was in pain. Her face was pale and covered with beads of perspiration.

Suddenly Sacagawea grabbed her stomach. She doubled over in pain. Her husband just sat back and watched as Captain Clark rushed to her side. "She's burning up with fever," he said. "Help me get her inside the tent."

Clark and York lifted Sacagawea and took her inside the tent. In order to reduce her fever, Clark needed some leeches. He sent York out to the swampy area by the river to find some of the slimy creatures. They would be placed on Sacagawea's arms to suck out the bad blood that was causing her illness. This was the only way he knew to help her at this time.

The very next morning she was up preparing food and caring for her baby as if nothing had ever been wrong with her. Her husband was not going to make any special concessions just because she was sick.

Clark was angry when he saw her up. "I told you to rest. Why are you doing this?" He touched her forehead. It was even hotter than it had been the night before. "Move her to my quarters. It's more sheltered from the weather," Clark instructed the men. It had started raining the night before, and he didn't want Sacagawea to get any sicker than she already was. And he knew that by moving her to his quarters, she would be away from that insufferable husband of hers.

"Here, drink this," coaxed Lewis as he held a cup up to her lips. It contained some water that York had gotten from the sulfur springs which was close by. Lewis also stirred in some opium and a mixture of ground bark that Sacagawea had taught him to make during the early days of their journey.

Captain Clark entered. "How is she?" he asked.

"Not much better. No wonder with that lazy, sorry man that claims to be her husband. He refuses to help her in any way and insists that she continue to wait on him. She must get some rest. We need her or we will not be able to convince the Shoshones to give us the horses we need," Lewis replied.

"The fever has made her delirious," Captain Clark admonished. "If she dies, it will be because of that devil of a husband of hers."

"Her pulse is irregular and there is twitching of her fingers and arms. She complains about pain in her lower abdomen," Lewis said. Both men assumed that it was probably due to her monthly cycle combined with some sort of infection. They would keep a close watch over her until she was better.

Lewis let it be known that Sacagawea would have plenty of food, medicine and rest for the next few days. She began to feel better after the second day.

"Oh, I'm happy to see you are better today," chided Charbonneau. He had already checked to make sure Lewis and Clark were nowhere in sight. "Since you are doing so well and since your friends are not here to protect you, why don't you get up and go into the woods to gather some of those wild apples I saw and cook them for my dinner. They would be very tasty, and being the good squaw that you are, I am sure you would want to do this for your loving husband." He smiled wickedly when he saw her wince when he called her a squaw. He may not be able to hit her but he still knew how to hurt her.

It took every ounce of strength that Sacagawea had to get up off her mat. She staggered into the woods and gathered the apples from the nearby woods. When Lewis and Clark returned, she was sitting by the fire, stirring the apples and feeding Little Pomp.

"What are you doing out of bed?" Lewis demanded. "I gave strict orders that you were to rest for a few days until you are better." He already knew the answer to his question. Charbonneau had decided that she was well enough to wait on him once again and they had not been there to stop him. He was way too lazy to take care of himself.

"I'm going to take care of that toad once and for all," shouted Clark. "Charbonneau, where are you? I'm going to tear you limb from limb!"

"Relax," Lewis said. "If we make him too angry he may just take Sacagawea and anything else he wants and leave. That would leave us with no means to get the horses from the Shoshones. You know how crazy he is!"

Clark cooled down a little before he caught up with Charbonneau. He didn't punch him out like he wanted to but he did give him a good tongue lashing about his treatment of Sacagawea. There was little doubt in the man's mind that this was his last chance. The next time, Clark just might kill him as he threatened!

In time, Sacagawea began to get better. Lewis, Clark and the other men of the expedition did everything within their power to help her make a full recovery. They brought her food and medicines. They entertained Little Baptiste so she could get the rest she needed. And most importantly, they kept her husband occupied elsewhere so she could have some peace and quiet!

A strong, permanent bond was created among Sacagawea and both Lewis and Clark because of the care they gave her during her illness. In exchange, she would perform many valuable services for them which would help to ensure the success of the expedition.

CHAPTER 14
ALMOST HOME

"I thought we'd never get our gear around the falls," lamented Clark as the last wagon was brought around the bend. They had spent an entire month bringing the canoes and supplies around the falls. They could hardly believe that they once thought these falls were the most beautiful sight they had ever seen. Now all the members of the Corps of Discovery saw when they looked at the falls was the sweat, calluses and sore muscles that they had endured just to get around them. They were anxious to proceed on the next leg of their journey west.

A few miles upstream from the falls, they were finally able to put their canoes into the water and paddle. The going was difficult because the currents were very strong. "Let's walk along the shore for a while longer," suggested

Lewis. "It will lighten the load and make our progression upstream much easier."

Clark agreed. Four men took to shore. "Look. I think we have some company," one of the men shouted. "Look at these willow shelters. And here, these are the tracks of horses."

Upon closer inspection, it was decided that this area had recently been an Indian camp. They all said a silent prayer that the camp had belonged to the Shoshones.

"They must have been spying on us as we moved around the falls," Clark said. "I don't see any signs of them now."

When Sacagawea arrived, she looked around and smiled. She was home at last! "These shelters were built by the Shoshones," she said. "See where the bark is stripped from these pine trees? They used the sap and soft part of the wood for food." She began to see landmarks that had been stored away in her memory for so many years. Yes, she was finally home!

Although search parties were sent out to find the Indians that were spying on them, none could be found. But they were there. They didn't even attempt to hide their tracks. It was as if they wanted the explorers to know they were there. It reminded Sacagawea of the game of hide and seek that she had played with her brother,

Cameahwait, and friend, Jumping Fish, that afternoon so long ago.

"Look up over that ridge," exclaimed Lewis. "Those must be fires set by the Indians to alert other tribes that we are in the area."

"Put the flags up on the canoes so the Indians will know that we are not an enemy tribe," suggested Clark. They also began leaving bits of clothing, paper and linen tape along the trail to let the Shoshones know that they were white men on a peace mission, not a raiding party.

The Shoshones saw the signs. The Shoshones saw the white men. But the white men did not see any of the Shoshones!

"I wish they would show themselves," lamented Clark. "It would certainly be nice to have some of those horses they have to help get us around these difficult rapids."

"Yes, it would be nice," Lewis replied, slapping at something in the air buzzing around his head. "These pests are nearly driving me out of my mind!" The pests he referred to were the mosquitoes, eye gnats and prickly pear that heavily populated the area. "They are worse than any three curses that Egypt ever had to endure!" he wailed.

As they were marching along the rugged terrain one day, Lewis looked up and discovered an Indian on horseback about two miles away. The native was coming towards them. He observed him through his glass and decided that the Indian's dress, unsaddled horse, and bow and quiver of arrows identified him as a Shoshone based on Sacagawea's description of her tribe.

Lewis was overjoyed and immediately unloosened the blanket from his pack. In the manner of friendship known by previous Indian tribes he had encountered, he grabbed two corners of his blanket and waved it in the air three times. The brave did not come any closer.

Fearing the native would leave, Lewis quickly took some beads, a looking glass and some other trinkets out of his bag and with Officers McNeal and Shields, approached unarmed towards him.

When they got about 200 paces away, the Indian began to back away. Lewis signaled for the other two men to stand still but Shields continued moving towards the native.

"Tab-ba-bone," Lewis shouted as he held the trinkets up for the Indian to see. He rolled up his sleeve so the white skin of his arm was showing. "Tab-ba-bone," he shouted again. This he knew meant "white men" in the Shoshone language. Sacagawea had taught the men some Shoshone words just in case something like this happened. He continued to approach the Indian very slowly. Shields also continued his forward movement.

Just when Lewis thought he would be able to make contact with the Indian, the brave turned his horse about, gave him the whip, and leapt the creek, disappearing in the willow bush.

"Well, there goes our hope of getting horses for the remainder of the trip," Lewis complained. "Why didn't you stop when I signaled you to?" Lewis demanded of Shields.

"I swear, I didn't see your signal. I was watching the Indian so closely that I didn't look to see what you two were doing," Shields lamented. "If I had, I certainly would have stopped. I know how badly we need those horses. I'm sorry."

After this encounter, Lewis attached a small United States flag to a pole which McNeal carried as they walked and planted in the ground when they halted or made camp.

As they labored along the treacherous river, they spied a tremendous bluff. The earth was blood red. "This is where we got the red clay that the Shoshone women use to paint pottery and other items," Sacagawea said. "For the Shoshones, red stands for peace." She touched the red rose on the bag her mother had made for her a lifetime ago. It had been a great source of comfort and peace for her during those long, lonely years.

"Man, look at all those rattlesnakes!" one of the men shouted. The cliff with the red clay was literally swarming with the serpents. "How in the world did you get the clay out of there without getting bitten?"

Sacagawea laughed. "Some of the girls were in charge of pushing the snakes to the back of the cliff while the women quickly gathered the clay in pots. We used fiery torches to drive them back. It was very dangerous and the snakes sometimes got close enough to bite us. We had to be really careful! Needless to say, this was not our favorite thing to do! But the red paint was essential to our people for decorations and religious purposes. And remember, the Shoshone tribe came from the Snake, so they are our ancestors. We believe that gives us some protection from their bites."

With each passing day, the area became more and more familiar to Sacagawea. She began to recognize places that she had traveled to as a child. She was even able to show the captains a shortcut through the mountains at one point.

"Stop!" Sacagawea shouted one day as the boats rounded a bend in the river. She sat frozen in place, pointing to some rocks at the edge of the water. "This is where I was hiding when I was kidnapped by the Hidatsa Tribe. I must go see if my people are still here."

They pulled the canoes up to the edge of the river. Sacagawea jumped out and ran towards her childhood home, hoping beyond hope that the family she thought she had lost forever would be there.

When none of her people could be found, Sacagawea wept. "Look, there are markings here. And the campfires are still smoldering. Here are some footprints. They must be close by. Please help me find them," she cried.

Lewis and Clark immediately sent out a search party. Not only were they anxious to help Sacagawea find her family, they were desperate for horses by this time, and their food supply was once again running low. Their clothing was nothing more than flea infested strips of material. Most of them had been going barefoot for weeks and they definitely needed some type of shoes to cover their bruised, bleeding feet. They knew that the Shoshones were not far away. Hopefully the natives would be able to help the explorers with all of their needs.

CHAPTER 15
A Happy Reunion

After several days of seeing signs they knew were definitely left by the Shoshones, a search party came upon a small group of Shoshone women. The braves were on a hunting expedition and the women were at a base camp, cooking and caring for the members of the hunting party.

At first the women were frightened by the sudden appearance of the white men for they had never seen white men before. One woman fled as soon as she saw them. The two remaining women, one old woman and the other a girl of about twelve, seated themselves on the ground and held down their heads as if they knew their fate was death. Lewis quickly produced gifts for the women so they would know that he and the others were friendly. He gave them the usual medals, mirrors and beads, but also presented them with something they had never seen before, corn which he had brought with him from the Mandans back east. The women were amazed by the colorful vegetable and smiled widely when they sniffed and tasted the hard, sweet kernels. They had never tasted anything like it before. When he presented them with an American flag, they stared in awe. They had never seen such beautiful fabric before. Their fabrics had always consisted of animal skins or rough fabrics they had woven themselves.

Once the women realized the explorers were not going to kill them, they allowed Lewis to use vermillion to paint their cheeks, an emblem of peace for the Shoshones.

Eventually, the group Sacagawea was with arrived. Sacagawea stepped forward. She greeted the Shoshones in their native tongue. She convinced them that the party had come in peace as witnessed by the gifts they bore. She finally talked them into taking the group to their chief so they could begin bargaining for the horses they would need to continue their journey west.

Just then, a group of Shoshone women came out of the woods carrying baskets of berries. One of them stopped short, stared at Sacagawea for a moment and dropped her basket to the ground. She screamed! Sacagawea looked up, saw the woman and started running towards her.

Both women shrieked with joy as they fell crying into each others' arms. Sacagawea had found her old friend, Yellow Flower. They had never expected to see each other again.

The group proceeded towards the camp and eventually ran into a party of about sixty warriors on horseback, racing towards them at full speed. When they arrived, Lewis approached them with the American flag. The braves embraced Lewis affectionately, saying "Ah-hi-e, ah-hi-e," which according to Sacagawea meant, "I am much pleased, I am much rejoiced."

The Shoshone tribe had been living on berries, roots and small game when the expedition found them. The previous spring they had been raided by the Pahkees tribe who had killed many of their people and stolen their buffalo skin teepees. They were in dire need of many of the things that the white men had, so they were willing to talk about trading their horses for them.

Imagine their surprise when Lewis, some of his men and the interpreters entered the wooden hut of the chief and saw Clark already sitting there in a white robe with white shells tied in his red hair. He had gotten there a few hours ahead of the others and was well on his way to making friends with the natives. No wonder the warriors had been so friendly! Clark had been showering them with gifts and through Charbonneau had told them of many more gifts yet to come.

Lewis and his men joined the group, and the men smoked and passed the pipe around as a sign of peace. After smoking the pipe, the real bartering began.

When Sacagawea entered the hut, she started screaming, "Cameahwait! Cameahwait!" Tears were streaming down her face as she ran up and hugged the chief.

The rest of the members of the expedition looked at each other in amazement. Was this a Shoshone custom they were not aware of?

Were they supposed to shout those strange words and run up and hug the chief? They weren't sure what they were supposed to do.

After a few moments, Charbonneau was able to decipher what was being said. He relayed his discovery to Drouillard and Drouillard in turn relayed the information to Lewis and Clark. "The chief is Sacagawea's brother. They haven't seen each other since she was kidnapped by the Hidatsa tribe many years ago. They each thought the other one was dead," they said in turn.

When his father had been killed, Cameahwait had become the chief of the Shoshones. Sacagawea was truly a lucky charm for the expedition. How could Chief Cameahwait deny his own long lost sister the horses they needed in order to complete their mission? They knew Sacagawea was Shoshone but they didn't know she was a Shoshone princess. What a pleasant surprise!

After a very emotional reunion, the bartering began once again. They finally closed the deal after much give and take on both sides. Lewis and Clark were able to secure the twenty-nine horses they needed in order to get over the Rocky Mountains, and the Shoshones got food, guns and ammunition they needed in order to survive.

The pipe was passed once again, this time using the tobacco that Lewis and Clark had brought with them from the Mandans. The chief even provided the party with wooden huts to sleep in overnight. How nice to have a real roof over their heads after spending so many months in makeshift tents!

Sacagawea, Cameahwait, Yellow Flower and the others talked way into the night, reminiscing about the days of their youth, before the Hidatsas raided their village, changing their lives forever.

Later that night as Sacagawea headed for the hut that she, Baptiste and Charbonneau would share for the night, she overheard some of the Shoshone braves talking. She couldn't believe her ears! They were planning to ambush the party and steal the horses back!

Sacagawea was infuriated! She headed straight for Cameahwait's hut and demanded to see him. No woman had ever dared to demand anything from a brave in the Shoshone village before, especially not the chief! And no one, man or woman, had ever dared to talk to Cameahwait so sharply!

"What do you mean planning to steal from these people who saved my life and have given our people the tools they need in order to survive?" Sacagawea demanded from her brother. She then proceeded to tell him what she had overheard.

He feigned innocence of the plot and assured her that they were safe from an attack by the Shoshones. If indeed he had planned the attack, he thought better of it after Sacagawea finished with him. Once again she had helped the Captains and the other members of the expedition.

"I bet she stays here with her people," Clark moaned that night as he and Lewis recorded the events of the day. "I wouldn't blame her if she did."

"She would surely be missed," Lewis agreed. "But what does she have to look forward to besides a life with that stupid, hateful man she married? However, I have the feeling that Sacagawea is happy wherever she is just as long as she has food for her belly and a few trinkets to decorate her body."

Lewis was right. Sacagawea had had a taste of freedom, and she liked it. She had no intentions of staying with the Shoshones where she would be little more than a slave again. Besides, Charbonneau would never let her take Little Baptiste with her, and she would never leave her child!

When the expedition was finally prepared to leave, Sacagawea was ready to go with them. She was happy to have seen her family and friends, but she had a new family now – the men of the Corps of Discovery.

CHAPTER 16
OLD TOBY

The captains went to Chief Cameahwait once again. "Where did you get the shells that you braided in my hair?" Clark asked. "They look like the shells of sea creatures."

Chief Cameahwait picked up one of the shells lying on the ground beside him. "We traded with the Nez Perce Indians for them several years ago. Their village is on the other side of the mountain, beside the Great Sea you are searching for," he said. "You will need a guide to get there. I will send Old Toby with you. He has made the journey many times."

"The Shoshones tell me the Salmon River is not navigable. I understand that it is very rocky and the currents are extremely dangerous. We'll have to take an overland route," Lewis said to the other members of the expedition when he returned from his meeting with Chief Cameahwait. "Take the canoes to the lake and sink them. I don't want them to be washed away by a storm or used for firewood by the Indians. We'll need them for our return trip."

Clark added, "If the Nez Perce trail is good enough for their women and children to travel across, then our men should be able to do it with ease."

A group of men began sinking the canoes in the lake, being careful to mark the location of each boat on a tree by the lake. Others proceeded to load their supplies on the horses. As they worked, they were thinking that the remainder of the journey would be easy. Little did they know the dangers that they were preparing to encounter.

With Old Toby leading the way, the explorers began their descent down the side of the North Fork. They were followed by Shoshone braves and even a few women and children. It was like a party to the Shoshones! They sang and danced as they followed the crew.

When they met up with the rest of the crew, the Indians saw York. They had never seen such black skin and curly hair in their lives. This was much more interesting than the skin of the white men! After their initial shock wore off, they curiously came to York and began rubbing his arms as if to remove the black paint. They rubbed his curly hair. Some of the women, not being shy about such things, began to flaunt their bodies in front of York, hoping to gain his approval.

York looked at the others with a big smile on his face and said, "I can't help it. Women just find me sexy!" This had happened at almost every Native American camp they had encountered on their journey and it never failed to please him. He was totally unaware of the fact that the novelty of his skin coloring was what had made many of the natives willing to trade with the white explorers as they traveled west.

The men had recently killed a few deer and thrown their entrails on the ground. As soon as the near starving Shoshones saw this, they fell on the ground, gouging their stomachs with every morsel they could find. York was momentarily forgotten. Understanding the plight the natives were in, the crew brought out another deer and presented it to the Indians. They were extremely pleased with the deer and happily carried it back to their camp as the explorers proceeded west.

Within a few days, the members of the expedition found themselves in a precarious position. The mountain walls were extremely close to the creek on both sides, making the trail very narrow and dangerous. They had to travel very carefully along the steep mountain walls.

Several of the horses lost their footing and were seriously injured. Their last thermometer was broken in one of those falls. That seemed to be an omen for what was going to happen next.

"Oh no, it's raining," whined Charbonneau. "As if the path weren't slippery enough already. We will never get out of here alive."

"Stop complaining," admonished Drouillard. "We've managed so far, and we'll do it again. We haven't come this far to give up."

The rain turned to sleet and the sleet turned to snow. "It's time to stop," called Clark. "We don't want any more injured horses or people. It's far too dangerous for us to continue under these conditions. Besides, it will be dark in a few hours and we'd just as soon go ahead and get things set up."

Everyone in the party dismounted and began unpacking. The camp was set up on the jagged rocks. There'd be no good night's sleep that night for any of the weary travelers.

Upon waking the next morning, the party was horrified to find everything frozen or wet. The ground was covered with snow. The going would be dangerous, but it would be even worse to stay where they were.

"Let's go," shouted Lewis. "If we can make it over the crest and down the side of that mountain, Old Toby says we'll be at the village of the Nez Perce Indians. There we can get food and shelter."

The group grudgingly packed up their gear and prepared to leave. The going got even tougher as they headed towards the crest of the mountain. It was a lot further than it looked. Their food supply had become almost nonexistent. There was virtually no game to hunt at this elevation. The possibility of starving was once again added to their list of woes.

Clark, Old Toby and several others scouted ahead of the party. "I'm going to name this creek Hungry Creek," Clark exclaimed. "I'm hungry enough to eat a horse! We need to go ahead and build a fire so the rest of the guys can at least warm up when they get here."

The next day, a hunting party was sent out. At this point, finding food was more important than proceeding on their journey west. The only thing they saw was an old stray horse. "Well, I said I was hungry enough to eat a horse," Clark said, eyeing the old hag hungrily.

"It's better than starving," replied Old Toby. The horse was shot, cleaned and cooked. Old Toby knew which parts to eat and helped the white men find the tastier morsels. It wasn't bad as long as they didn't think about what they were eating.

As they journeyed over the treacherous path, they spied a river in the valley below. "That river flows from the Missouri River through a gentle valley. It is about a four day trip by horse," Old Toby said nonchalantly.

Clark shrieked, "Why didn't you tell us that, old man? We've traveled all this time through treacherous mountain paths, risking our lives at every turn. And now you calmly tell us that we could have had an easy journey lasting only four days. What were you thinking?"

"But that isn't my fault. I must have missed one of the markers somewhere along the trail," Old Toby replied defensively. "I haven't made this journey for many years and things have changed. Besides, we started our journey from our hunting camp. If we had left from our home village, I would have been better able to find our way. The weather conditions didn't help either. I'm sorry."

Old Toby led them through the valley and up the side of the mountain. He lost his way once but was able to regain his bearings the next day. Game was so scarce that they had to sacrifice all of their colts for food before they reached the other side of the mountains.

It took eleven days for the men to journey through the Bitterroot Mountains. "These are the most terrible mountains I ever beheld," lamented one of the explorers. It was indeed an unpleasant journey for all involved. Things had to get better soon.

CHAPTER 17
CHIEF TWISTED HAIR

Lewis never lost sight of his mission despite the horrible events that had taken place since they had left the Shoshone village. He discovered and was able to describe species of birds, including varied thrush, grouse, jays and a black woodpecker that still carries his name. The party finally reached the camp of the Nez Perce Indians. Although destitute themselves, the Nez Perce Indians were willing to share what little they had with the explorers.

"All we have is roots and salmon to eat," Chief Twisted Hair told Lewis and Clark. "We will be happy to share with you." After living off of horse meat for several days, the men were happy to have a change, even if it was only fish and roots.

Sacagawea came in with a big smile on her face one morning. In her hands she held some flower buds. "These will make a delicious meal," she told Clark. She started preparing the dish of buds she had carried in her hands and pockets. The aroma from the buds was fantastic as they simmered over the fire. When they were finally done, the members of the expedition were pleasantly surprised to find that the buds were actually very tasty. They all enjoyed a new, special treat that evening.

Slowly the explorers began to regain their strength. They learned many things from the Nez Perce tribe. In exchange for their hospitality, Lewis and Clark administered some ointment to help the Indians who had developed problems with their eyes. As fishermen, they spent so much time on the water that their eyes were damaged from the sun's reflection day after day, year after year. The ointment seemed to help clear up the eye infections although they couldn't repair the damage done by the sun's reflection on the water. The Indians were very thankful.

Sacagawea soon learned how lucky the Corps of Discovery had been once again. As Sacagawea and an old Nez Perce woman named Watkuweis were talking one afternoon, Watkuweis said, "You know that my people wanted to kill your party when they first saw you coming. They wanted your weapons."

"What do you think made them change their minds?" Sacagawea inquired.

"I did," Watkuweis replied. "I was captured by the Blackfoot Indians many years ago. They traded me to a white trader for supplies. He treated me very well and eventually returned me to my people. I convinced Chief Twisted Hair that the white people had treated me fairly and that we should show them the same courtesy. For some reason, he agreed."

Chief Twisted Hair surprised the captains the next day with some news that they had waited a long time to hear. "The Great Water that you are searching for is only two weeks towards the setting sun," he said as he pointed towards the west.

"You're kidding!" Clark said. He slapped Lewis on the back and threw back his head in laughter. "I never thought we'd make it. How do we get there?"

"You'll need canoes," Chief Twisted Hair responded. "It's much easier to travel on the river than it is to travel overland."

Let's get started," Lewis said. "But what will we do with the horses? We will need them for our return trip."

"Leave them with me," Chief Twisted Hair said. "We will care for them until you return. You don't have to worry about us eating them because our tribe doesn't believe in eating horse flesh. Our diet consists of salmon and other fish we catch in the river. We occasionally eat elk and deer if we are lucky enough to kill one."

The party began building the canoes that they would need for the last leg of their journey. The job was made easier because the Indians chipped in and helped.

After a few days, the canoes were finally ready. The explorers excitedly set out on their journey down the Clearwater River.

As they reached the Snake River, they met with another Indian tribe. The natives were on a hunting expedition and were camping by the river. The braves of the tribe greeted them.

"What do you have to eat?" Lewis asked one of the Indians through his interpreters. As usual, their food supply was low.

"Salmon and dogs," the Indians replied. "We had some whale meat but it's almost gone. A large whale washed up on shore about a week ago and we got meat from it but we aren't willing to share that."

"We're sick of salmon," the men yelled back. "There's salmon for breakfast, salmon for lunch and salmon for dinner. Anything would be a welcome change."

Lewis purchased some dogs from the Indians for the explorers to eat and eventually talked them out of a little bit of the whale blubber. He didn't waste any more time talking with the Indians. He was too anxious to see the whale that had washed up on shore.

A few days later as they were paddling down the river, Clark told everyone to stop talking. He strained his ears. "Listen," he said softly. "Do you hear that?"

The others strained to hear what Clark was talking about. Suddenly they started yelling and shouting. They had heard it too. They finally heard the roaring of the ocean waves against the shore, a sound they had waited for what seemed like an eternity to hear. They were finally within reach of their destination.

CHAPTER 18
REACHING THE PACIFIC

It wasn't long before the party caught their first glimpse of the Pacific Ocean. From his view at the top of the mountain, Clark declared, "From this point I beheld the grandest and most pleasing prospects which my eyes ever surveyed, in my front a boundless Ocean; a most romantic appearance."

The others on the expedition quickly agreed, especially those like Sacagawea who had never seen an ocean before. There was nothing but beautiful, rolling waves washing against the rocky shore for as far as their eyes could see.

When the excitement of finally reaching their destination wore off, the members of the expedition had to make some major decisions.

"We must select a site for our winter camp," Lewis told the party one morning. "Winter is coming and we will not be able to pass back over the mountains until the spring thaw gets here."

"Yes, and we must be able to kill some animals to obtain some furs to make clothes. Ours are so tattered and flea infested that we will freeze to death if we don't itch to death first," one of the other men exclaimed.

"There are several sites that we can choose from," said Clark. "I guess it's only fair that we discuss the suitable sites and put the matter to a vote."

"Well, I think we should build our camp overlooking the ocean," Charbonneau suggested. "It's such a glorious view from that bluff over there."

"It's not protected enough," Clark said. "The winter winds coming off the ocean would blow us away and the wind chill would be unbearable."

"It should be on the south side of the river," York offered. "There are plenty of elk in the area so we would have a good supply of food. And we could use our time to make new clothes from their skins. There would have protection from the winds coming off the ocean as well."

"There are also many roots and plants that we can eat in that area," Sacagawea added.

"What in the world do you two have to do with it?" asked Charbonneau sarcastically. "You are just an old black slave and an Indian squaw. You don't have any say in the matter."

"Wrong!" Clark boomed. "Both Sacagawea and York have proven to be very important members of this expedition. They have just as much right to help decide where we spend the winter as anyone else in the group."

"That's right. They've done more than some members of this group," added Lewis, looking straight at Charbonneau. "I say they have a vote. How do the rest of you feel about York and Sacagawea having a vote?"

Except for Charbonneau, all of the members of the party agreed. So for the first time in American history, a black man and a woman were given the right to vote.

After discussing a few other possible sites, the group voted to build their winter quarters on the south side of the Columbia River, the site favored by both Sacagawea and York. It was close to the Clatsop Indian village so they called it Fort Clatsop.

With that decision behind them, they were anxious to get to the next business at hand – the beached whale that the Indians had told them about. They walked down the beach searching for the huge beast. Most of them had never seen anything of that proportion before. But their trip was in vain. The only thing left of the whale was its skeleton, but the group was quite impressed by its size. It measured 105 feet from head to tail. Between the Indians and the birds, it had been picked clean. The explorers were a little disappointed but not surprised.

By this time, Little Baptiste was toddling around. Clark never tired of watching the child play and explore his surroundings. He had watched the child grow from a tiny infant to a chubby toddler during the past year and felt a special kinship to the little boy.

"Look at him bounce around!" Clark exclaimed one day. "He just bounces from one place to another, never tiring. Anyone with that much energy deserves a special name. I think I'll call him Pomp. Baptiste is just too stuffy a name for an active little boy."

"You are so right. Pomp suits him," replied Sacagawea. From that day forward, Baptiste was known as Pomp by all of the explorers except of course, Charbonneau.

Christmas was a meager affair that year. For the men of the Corps of Discovery, it was just another day. However, they did think of Little Pomp. It was his first Christmas, and the men wanted to be sure that it was memorable. They had plenty of spare time so they busily whittled little toys from pieces of wood as they sat by the fire at night. They worked on them for several weeks. By the time Christmas arrived, Little Pomp had quite a stash of toys to play with. He had a wonderful time going from one man to the next, his eyes glistening with wonder at the treasures they showered upon him. Yes, Christmas was wonderful for little Pomp.

Sacagawea had squirreled away some of the fruit she had dried during the summer and fall. She used it to make sweet cakes for Pomp and the members of the expedition.

"Ma, look!" Pomp squealed as he received yet another toy from Clark. It was a shiny round object Clark had removed from one of his broken instruments. It bounced and tumbled and rolled. Little Pomp chased it around as fast as his chubby little legs could carry him, laughing with delight as he ran. He grabbed another cake and popped it into his mouth as he ran by his mother. Then it was back to his game.

Sacagawea was not really familiar with Christmas traditions but she had been exposed to them when she lived in the Mandan village. With the exception of the cakes she had made, she had no other plans to celebrate. She was however delighted to see that Pomp was having such a wonderful day.

The fiddles were brought out and the music began! The group sang, clapped their hands and stomped their feet along with the music.

Clark presented Sacagawea with a beautiful necklace made from the same blue beads as the belt he had given her earlier in the journey. What a handsome set they made. Sacagawea's smile was almost as large as Little Pomp's.

Charbonneau was livid! He hadn't planned to give anyone a gift, not even his young son. He thought the whole gift giving thing was ridiculous. But how dare Clark give a gift to Sacagawea! She was his wife! He fussed and fumed and sulked all night, but he didn't hit her. He was still afraid that Clark would hold true to his word to kill him if he left another mark on Sacagawea. He wasn't willing to take a chance on it, so he suffered in silence.

CHAPTER 19
LITTLE BLUE FROG

Captain Lewis spent the winter organizing the many maps, charts and drawings that he had collected on his journey west. President Jefferson would be very pleased with the wealth of information that the Corps of Discovery would present to him when they returned back east. They had successfully found a route joining the east coast to the west coast. They had been able to identify numerous plants and animals that had never before been seen by white men. And most importantly, they had established positive relationships with the many different Indian tribes they met along the way. Yes, President Jefferson would be pleased, even if they didn't find any woolly mammoths or lava spewing volcanoes along the way.

Clark could neither confine himself to the fort they had built nor the area around it. He was an explorer by nature so he spent the cold, winter days going out on hunts and adventures. He always came back with some interesting plant for Sacagawea to identify, a strange animal to talk about, or an exciting story to share with the rest of the group. He kept the entire party entertained with his glorious "finds".

"Captain Clark, the Clatsops have done it again"! exclaimed one of the members of the party. Living in a society where no one owned anything and everyone shared everything, the Clatsop Indians thought nothing of picking up tools and other knickknacks belonging to the explorers. Every few days the men of the Corps of Discovery would have to visit the Clatsop village to retrieve their items. Try as they might, the explorers couldn't get it through the Clatsops' minds that they shouldn't steal. To them, it wasn't stealing. They saw something they liked so they took it home with them.

"What did they get this time?" questioned Clark.

"They took my hatchet," the man replied. "I know the drill. I'll go pick it up and check for other items while I'm there. I think I know which one took it. He was hiding behind some bushes and didn't think I saw him. I put the hatchet down to move some limbs I had cut and when I turned back around, it was gone and so was he.

I'll be back shortly. It seems like they would catch on after a while."

Sacagawea used this time to play with her son, Pomp. She taught him simple games, helped him master several new words, and shared wonderful Shoshone stories with him that her mother had told her when she was a child.

One night as they sat by the fire, Little Pomp begged, "Li'l fog, Mama, Li'l fog!"

Sacagawea knew he wanted to hear his favorite story, a wonderful Shoshone tale about a little blue frog. In her wonderful, musical voice that sounded so like her mother's, Sacagawea began the story.

Once upon a time, there was a little blue frog. He lived in a large pond right in the middle of the forest with large, silvery fish, huge dragonflies, and of course, other frogs. But the other frogs didn't like the little blue frog because he wasn't green like them. He also had strange feet with webbed, sticky toes. The Little Blue Frog spent the summer sitting all by himself on his lily pad in the middle of the pond, eating his favorite food, big green flies! Any attempt he made at making friends with the other frogs was met with ridicule. He was indeed a very lonely little frog.

When the cold winter winds began to blow, Little Blue Frog did the same thing that his green cousins did. He swam down to the bottom of the pond and burrowed himself deep in the mud. There he slept the long, cold winter away, dreaming of a life filled with friends and laughter.

Spring came. All of the frogs were delighted to swim to the pond's surface and bask in the warm sunshine. As directed by 'Mother Earth', all of the frogs started singing their mating songs and Little Blue Frog naturally joined right in. What a fuss they made! Suddenly, all of the green frogs stopped singing. They had heard a new and different voice among them. It was without a doubt the most beautiful voice they had ever heard. Where in the world was it coming from? The green frogs just had to know!

They began searching far and wide for the source of the beautiful music. Their search led them straight to the Little Blue Frog. He was sitting all alone on his lily pad right in the middle of the pond, singing his little heart out. The other frogs were jealous. While the others stared at the Little Blue Frog, enjoying his beautiful voice, Little Blue Frog heard something. It was another beautiful voice that sounded much like his. He had to find the source of that music.

The Little Blue Frog immediately found the source of the music in a nice tree throwing shade on his lily pad in the middle of the big pond. Sitting on a branch high up in the tree, he saw a little blue frog with sticky, webbed feet! At first he thought he was just looking at his own reflection. However, when he sang his song, his reflection sang right back! He sang again. His reflection responded again. Little

Blue Frog had found his mate. From that day forward, he was a very happy little blue frog, sitting high up in the tree with his new mate. Little Blue Frog had finally found his place in this world.

You see, the Great Mystery had made the Little Blue Frog different from all the other frogs. He wasn't a green pond frog at all! He was a little blue tree frog. He wasn't even supposed to sit on a lily pad in the middle of the big pond day after day, eating big green flies. He was supposed to climb high up in the trees and sing so all of the animals on Earth could hear his beautiful voice.

From that day forward, the green pond frogs looked forward to hearing the little blue frog, his wife and all their little baby frogs singing their hearts out from their home high up in the tree."

As she told the story, she noticed a strange thing happening. The men sitting around the fire within hearing distance had stopped talking. They were listening to Sacagawea's story! They were able to understand just enough of the words to be able to follow along. They were so intrigued by the beautiful sing-song quality of Sacagawea's voice that they didn't seem to mind the fact that they didn't understand every word that was being said.

After she finished the story, York came up to her. With a tear in his eye, he said, "Sacagawea, you and I are like that little blue frog, aren't we? We are different from the rest of the group. You are Shoshone, and I am Black. But just like the little blue frog, we each have our place in the world and an important job to do while we are here."

Sacagawea smiled. York was right; they did have their place in the world, right here, helping these strong men make the New World a better place for all mankind.

EPILOGUE

The journey back east was not void of excitement. Twice the men had horses stolen by Indians while they were sleeping. Two Blackfoot Indians were killed in the subsequent fight when they snuck into camp one night and awakened some of the men in the party. Lewis and his men had to make a swift retreat down the Missouri River before the irate Blackfoot Indians were able to retaliate.

The Corps was delayed by deep snow on the Lolo Trail that went through the Bitterroot Mountains. Pomp became ill with a high fever and a swollen neck and throat. Thinking he had the mumps or tonsillitis, the captains applied poultices of wild onions and a plaster made of salve made from the resin of the long leaf pines, beeswax and bear's oil mixed together. It took Pomp about two and a half weeks to get better, about the same length of time that it took for the snow to subside.

One night a herd of buffalo were stampeding directly towards the sleeping campers. Clark's dog, Seaman, was able to head them off long enough for the explorers to safely get out of their way. Yes, things were quite exciting on their journey home.

Clark, along with the Charbonneau family and several others, explored the Yellowstone River area. They came across an unusual sandstone formation on the south shore of the river. Clark named the formation "Pompy's Tower". Clark etched his name under a protected overhand along with the date, July 25, which happened to be his birthday. This etching can still be seen today, protected by a piece of unbreakable glass. It is considered to be the only physical evidence left on the landscape by the Corps of Discovery. Clark also named a nearby creek "Baptiste's Creek" in honor of the child.

Towards the end of the expedition, a nearly blind corpsman, Pierre Cruzatte, accidentally shot Lewis in the hip. The wound caused Lewis problems for the rest of the journey.

Charbonneau, Sacagawea and Little Pomp were left with the Mandan Tribe where they were reunited with the rest of the wives. All of the explorers were paid $500.33, a horse, a voucher for 320 acres of land and a log house for their services on the journey. Charbonneau kept all of the cash and moved his large family into the log house.

He sold his land voucher to Clark for $100. Farming just wasn't in his blood. Clark wanted to take Pomp with him as his adopted son but it was decided that the child was too young to leave his mother. Six years later, Sacagawea gave birth to a daughter. She named her Lisette.

William Clark settled in Saint Louis where he became a public official and the Superintendent of Indian Affairs. Clark wrote a letter to Charbonneau stating that he was still interested in raising Pomp as his own child. He would educate him and treat him well. He also offered Charbonneau a piece of land, horses, hogs and cows if he wished to move to St. Louis. It was decided that Pomp would live with Clark, taking advantage of all he had to offer. Pomp was sent to boarding school at Clark's expense. Clark was later married and fathered several children of his own.

Pomp returned to the wilderness at age eighteen after completing his education. He met Prince Paul Wilhelm of Wuertemberg, Germany at one of the camps. Pomp intrigued the Prince and was taken back to Europe as the Prince's guest. Pomp enjoyed the aristocratic environment of the German court. For six years he lived the lifestyle of royalty, becoming fluent in four languages and acquainting himself with European Royalty. Pomp's exotic good looks and ability to communicate with people made him a prized guest at parties.

In 1829, Pomp came back to America and returned to the west where he hunted, trapped, guided and explored. He and Sacagawea were reunited in Wind River, Wyoming where she was living with her people. Pomp didn't stay long. He contracted "gold fever" and participated in the California Gold Rush. Apparently he didn't strike it rich because he was listed as a hotel clerk in Auburn, California in 1861. In 1866, he headed towards new gold discoveries in Montana with two companions. He died of pneumonia en route at the age of 61 and was buried in a remote cemetery in Danner, Oregon. His gravesite was entered into the National Register of Historic Places in 1973.

Meriwether Lewis was appointed Governor of Louisiana in 1807 by President Jefferson who was very pleased with the Corps of Discovery's findings. Lewis missed the challenge of leading a team of explorers through the wilderness. He was unlucky with women and turned to drink to fill the void. He died of two gunshot wounds, one to the head and one to the chest on October 11, 1809 in a Tavern called Grinder's Stand while on his way to Washington, DC. It has never been determined whether it was murder or suicide.

Sacagawea divorced Charbonneau and married in the Shoshone tribe, possible more than once. There she gave birth to many children. She told stories of her adventures with the white men's Corps of Discovery, becoming a legend among her people. She proudly wore the Jefferson Medal which had been presented to her by President Thomas Jefferson in honor of her contributions to the expedition led by Meriwether Lewis and William Clark.

Sacagawea spoke at a political meeting which led to the Fort Bridger Treaty. There an agreement was made between the Indian nations and the American government to strive to maintain peace among the Native Americans and the white settlers as they traveled west over the route charted by the Corps of Discovery.

Sacagawea is credited with reintroducing the Sun Dance Ceremony to the Shoshone people. She taught them how to plant and grow new crops. She also was very instrumental in acquiring rights for not only the Shoshone women, but for women all over the country.

Sacagawea died at Fork Washakie, Wyoming on April 9, 1884. She is believed to have been between ninety-five and one hundred years old when she died. She was living with her son, Basil, at the time of her death.* Her descendants live on, proud of the great, great-grandmother whose unselfish contributions, sacrifice and personal courage led to the discovery of a new land – the land west of the Mississippi River.

There are more statues, more schools, more parks, mountain peaks, rivers and lakes named for Sacagawea than for any other woman in American history. Because of the many contributions Sacagawea made during and after the expedition, the Secretary of the Treasury of the United States announced in July of 1998 that a likeness of Sacagawea would replace the image of Susan B. Anthony on the dollar coin, a fitting tribute to a truly amazing woman.

*Some historians claim that Sacagawea died at age twenty-four. Shoshone Woman and Sacagawea's other descendents support family lore that Sacagawea lived to be a very old woman.

About the Author

Sandra Taylor-Miller is a retired educator and an award winning author. She is a graduate of Atlantic Christian (Barton) College in Wilson, NC where she earned her BS in Early Childhood Education. She later received her Masters in Elementary Education from East Carolina University in Greenville, NC. Sandra taught grades Kindergarten through eighth grade during her thirty years of service to the Martin County Board of Education in North Carolina. She is a double recipient of *Who's Who Among American Teachers.*

Sandra's first book, *Are We There Yet? The Wright Brothers' National Memorial Park*, received the prestigious Willie Parker Peace History Book Award from the North Carolina Society of Historians, Inc. in 2004. This award was given to Mrs. Taylor-Miller for her "many valuable contributions to the collection, preservation and perpetuation of North Carolina's rich history".

Sandra and her husband, Roger, live in Williamston, North Carolina where she is a member of the Williamston Woman's Club, the Martin County Arts Council and the First Christian Church.